P9-DFO-727

EVeRYtHiNG
i know about
PaReNTiNG
i learned from
MY PuPPY

H. Norman Wright
Paintings by Jim Lamb

H
HARVEST HOUSE PUBLISHERS
EUGENE, OREGON

Everything I Know About Parenting I Learned from My Puppy

Copyright © 2002 by H. Norman Wright
Published by Harvest House Publishers
Eugene, Oregon 97402

   Library of Congress Cataloging-in-Publication Data
Wright, H. Norman.
   Everything I know about parenting I learned from my puppy / by H.Norman Wright ; paintings by Jim Lamb.
      p. cm.
   ISBN 0-7369-0649-5 (alk. paper)
   1.Parenting—Religious aspects—Christianity. I. Title.
   BV4529 .W73 2002
   248.8'45—dc21
                              2002002438

Artwork designs are copyrighted by Jim Lamb and may not be reproduced without the artist's permission. For information regarding art prints featured in this book, please contact:

Jim Lamb   For limited edition prints: For art cards and mini prints:
1604 217TH Place SE   Wild Wings, Inc.   Art in Motion
Sammamish, WA 98075   (800) 445-4833   (800) 663-1308
E-mail: Plainair2@attbi.com
Website: www.jimlambstudio.com

Design and production by Koechel Peterson & Associates, Minneapolis, Minnesota

Harvest House Publishers has made every effort to trace the ownership of all poems and quotes. In the event of a question arising from the use of a poem or quote, we regret any error made and will be pleased to make the necessary correction in future editions of this book.

Unless otherwise indicated, Scripture quotations are taken from the Holy Bible, New International Version®, Copyright © 1973, 1978, 1984 by the International Bible Society. Used by permission of Zondervan Publishing House. Scripture quotations marked NASB are from the New American Standard Bible®, © 1960, 1962, 1971, 1972, 1973, 1975, 1977 by The Lockman Foundation. Used by permission.

Printed in China

03 04 05 06 07 08 09 10 / IM / 10 9 8 7 6 5 4 3 2

Table of Contents

The Art of Puppies and Parenting

A PUPPY—JUST THE WORD ITSELF BRINGS to mind the image of a cute, frolicking, lovable bundle of fun with an inquisitive nose and mouth. There's nothing that elicits an "Ohhhh—isn't it cute" response better than that innocent-looking wiggly creature that's just beginning its journey into dog life. That is, nothing else other than an adorable baby—alert with an expression of wonder and marvel at a world just waiting to be explored.

Both are starting out ready to discover what life is all about. They're similar in a lot of ways.

Both need instruction—careful wisdom-filled teaching with the right balance of training.

And the owners of a puppy and the parents of a child are similar—each of them needs instruction—one to know how to teach their dog and the other how to parent their child.

So, does that mean if you get a puppy and have a baby you need to attend dog-training classes and parenting classes? Well… it is a good idea. After all, a well-trained dog is a delight, but if it's not trained…well, take my word for it. Neither you nor your neighbors would be happy campers. And raising a child! Well, of course we need some help. After all, who among us was ever taught how to parent! Most of us spent more time preparing to get our driver's license than we ever did preparing to be a parent. It's true. So we revert back to the way we were raised even though most of us vowed, "I'll never raise my kids the way I was raised." So classes would benefit us. But wait. Perhaps there's an easier way…like a shortcut.

It's simple, but workable. It's like having the best of both worlds. Raise a puppy before you have a baby. That's right. Raise a puppy first! I've even suggested this to couples I'm working with in premarital counseling. If they plan to be parents, buy a puppy and raise it. That's not all they'll need, but it's amazing what you learn by raising a puppy. Both go through the teething stage, don't they? Both have to be potty-trained, don't they? Both need to learn what to eat and what not to eat, don't they? Both need discipline, teaching, training, and to understand the meaning of the word "no," don't they? Of course they do—and much more. So, if you want to raise a well-adjusted child, raise a well-adjusted puppy.

Just imagine—instead of entering parenthood as an amateur and making all those mistakes on your child, make them on your puppy. (Well, maybe there is a better way of putting it.)

If a person can learn all about life in kindergarten (Robert Fulghum), why not learn all about parenting from our puppies? It's true! It works. It's effective. It's enjoyable. But you've got to be willing to learn. Keep an open mind. Take this information in and retain it. Lock it up and use it. It begins with us. After all, dog-training classes aren't for the dog. They're to show the owner how to train and teach their dog. Those owners who follow the teaching and apply it to their dogs have a wonderful experience. Those who don't have a constant frustration and a continuing power struggle as to who is going to be top dog or the leader of the pack. I've seen homes dominated and controlled by a dog. It's not a pretty sight. I've also seen parents controlled, manipulated, and dominated by their children. That's an even uglier sight. Neither needs to happen. So, let's see how our experiences with a puppy can help us parent our children in a loving and responsible way. ❧

A dog teaches a boy fidelity, perseverance,
and to turn around three times before lying down.

ROBERT BENCHLEY

Your Puppy's Brain

YES, IT'S TRUE. YOUR PUPPY DOES HAVE A BRAIN. BELIEVE IT OR NOT. Oh, I know there are times when you wonder. In some ways, it's like yours. The neurons in your brain have the same chemical composition as a dog's brain and the patterns of electrical activity are the same. How does that make you feel…knowing your brain has some similarities to your dog's?

Both people and pups have special areas of the brain set aside for special tasks. For example, vision is at the back of the brain for both and hearing is at the side, near the temples.

But there are some differences. Psychologists believe about 60 percent of the human brain is used for processing conscious thoughts, interpreting and creating language, and problem solving. Dog owners believe that 60 percent of their dog's brain is set aside to demonstrate the verb "to eat." ❧

A Message from Your Puppy

"HELLO. I'M YOUR PUPPY AND I WOULD LIKE TO SHARE SOMETHING WITH YOU. I've seen humans with bumper stickers that say, 'Born to shop.' Well, I was 'Born to sniff.' It's true. I'm not rude when I go up to a person and sniff. I'm not trying to embarrass you. You see and hear. Well, so do I, but the best way for me to identify something is through my nose. When I see another pup I greet him by sniffing. You keep a photo album to keep track of your travels. I can't do that. You visit places, but I visit odors. My nose is *sooo* good I can find illegal drugs, bombs, and people under the ground, water, or snow. I can sniff out termites, a drop of blood diluted by a gallon-and-a-half of water, and even certain cancers in a body. I don't mean to boast, but I have almost 195 million more smelling cells in my nose than the 5 million you do. Compared to humans, I'm olfactory gifted. You're olfactory challenged. Puppy power! Arf, Arf.

"Touch my nose. It should be damp. Touch your child's nose. If it's damp and running, you've got a problem. If mine is dry, I've got a problem.

"Why is my nose wet? Well, let me tell you a folktale. Remember the story of Noah's ark? Well, supposedly the two dogs Noah chose were patrolling the ark, checking up on everything the way dogs do. One day as they cruised through the ark, they discovered a coin-sized leak. One ran for help while the other plugged the hole with his nose. By the time Noah and the others got there to repair the hole, the dog was gasping for breath, and boy, did his nose hurt. But he did his job. And as the story goes, the wet nose is a badge of honor conferred on dogs by God in memory of what happened on the ark.

"Anyway, be thankful for my nose. I am." ❧

10

Surviving Puppyhood

PUPPIES ARE GREAT TEACHERS. THEY TEACH YOU PATIENCE AND CONSISTENCY. They train you to put things away, close doors, and never leave anything around you don't want chewed. They educate you to be on the alert, watch where you walk, and before they're potty-trained, never, ever walk through the house barefoot.

They teach you not to leave three dozen freshly baked cookies on the counter within their reach and then go outside for 20 minutes. If you do, they'll wolf them down. Ours did. That pile of flour, sugar, and (toxic to a dog) chocolate chips churned and fermented in his stomach all night. In the morning the vet taught *him* the meaning of binging and purging. Not a pretty sight.

Puppies frolic. They're mischievous…and they chew. Puppies were born to chew. (That built-in gene clicks in. There's no thinking, no discrimination, and if your scent is on it, it's even better.) After all, you're part of their pack and if your smell is on it, it must be important. Your child is different. It's not the smell that attracts them but when they watch you use something they're curious and want to not only discover what you're using, but follow your lead.

Puppies should come into the world with a sign on them "born to chew." If it moves, chew it. If it doesn't move, chew it. If it's soft, hard, pliable, brittle, dull, or bright, chew it! Your Ethan Allen Early American furniture could be modified to a new style—distressed!

Remember the first Christmas with your puppy? Especially the tree ornaments and how they tended to disappear? Fortunately, the green Christmas tree lightbulb that our golden retriever ate wasn't that expensive—only 79 cents. It was *much* less expensive than his mistress' glasses he had chewed up two days before. It was that episode that helped me make the decision to take out a medical insurance policy on the pup. This little investment has paid off quite well.

Remember that you'll survive puppyhood and its daily adventures and misadventures. We have, time after time—including the episode with the "shrinking" garden hose. It wasn't that we had failed to buy a pre-shrunk hose…it was a nice, long, 50-foot hose. It started shrinking while we were away on vacation. A neighbor came over each day to feed our puppy and water the flowers. After the third day, he was confused.

He said, "I could have sworn this hose was longer, but each day it seemed to be getting shorter." He was right. Every time he left, he also left the hose out. And as soon as the puppy saw it, he proceeded to chew off a six-foot hunk of hose and take off with it. It became shorter and shorter until I just threw it away.

I couldn't get upset at Sheffield, though. It wasn't his fault. He did what puppies are wired to do: If it's in sight, chew it. That's the universal doggie rule. You can't change it, so don't try to fight it. Just put away the hose.

Children aren't much different. They'll get into your cleaning materials, grab Aunt Fanny's favorite vase, chew on a leaf from your exotic fern, and even eat the puppy chow. It's not their fault. If it's there, they want to touch it, feel it, throw it, or eat it. That's what little children do…if we don't put it out of reach. ❧

A BLESSING FOR A CHILD'S NEW PET

May this little pet bring pleasure and
make the cloudiest days seem bright

May this little pet bring comfort and warmth
when the world feels cold and lonely

May this little pet teach patience and caring—
the foundation of all earthly peace

May this little pet foster understanding through
the universal language of life and love

May this little pet grow along with this child
from season to season and year to year

May this little pet create love everywhere
through its sheer being in our lives

JOANNA EMERY

Seven Black Puppies

A CLOSE FRIEND OF MINE WROTE THE FOLLOWING ABOUT HIS EXPERIENCE WITH PUPPIES:

Sherry and I went on a pheasant hunt with one of our friends and saw how great it was having a dog to hunt over. His yellow lab was one of the greatest hunting dogs she had ever had the privilege to see working in the field. We both thought it would be great to have one as mine had died years ago. We also thought it would be great for our son Jesse to have and help train. Harold, the lab's owner, told us that his dog would be having puppies in the near future and would let us know when they arrived. The puppies were born and we were so excited about seeing them, we drove up to Victorville to look at them. What we weren't ready for was Harold had another litter with one of his other hunting dogs…a black lab with the cutest black puppies you will ever see (but all lab puppies are cute and irresistible).

Sherry looked up at me with the biggest brown eyes and said, "Can I have one…please?" I tried to explain to her that we were going to be getting one of the yellow ones…then she said  "please" again and was holding this one female that cuddled up to her and purred like a cat. I said, "Sweetie, if it will make you happy, sure." She was so excited because she had always wanted a black lab. We took her home that night. Then we picked up the yellow boy lab five weeks later. Molly, our female, came into her first heat and I assured her that Buck, our boy dog, was way too young to know anything about making babies…Sherry kept telling me she thought the dog was putting on a lot of weight, and I assured her it meant nothing…Molly had seven beautiful black puppies last Wednesday.

Sherry never saw the puppies. She died the Saturday before and is now in the presence of Jesus. Forty-three years is awfully early to die, but cancer has no regard for age. As she lay in the ICU ward breathing oxygen, she asked to see Molly one more time. So she waddled in looking like she was going to give birth at any moment. Molly got up on the bed, and she and Sherry hugged.

Two days later Sherry was gone. It was a brief marriage. Only three-and-a-half years, but the honeymoon never ended. This is what her husband Dale said in his letter about her at the memorial service:

What Sherry and I had in the three-and-a-half years together was packed with so many memories…we thought we were making up for things we missed out on in the past, but we didn't realize we were doing things for the future that we wouldn't have together. We had a

wonderful time and life together and neither of us would have changed it for anything. I would do it all over again in a second if God gave me that chance…If there is one thing from my experience that could be passed on to any couple, it would be to enjoy every minute that you have together…as it could be your last.

I'm sure that Sherry is enjoying the playful antics of those adorable pups from a heavenly perspective. ❧

New Life

A NUMBER OF YEARS AGO I BURNED OUT. I overdid. One day I woke up and could care less about going to a speaking engagement, or teaching (which I love to do), or even going fishing (which I *really* love to do). I didn't care about much of anything. I had no energy. So I went to my doctor. His advice in non-medical terms was, "It's like a one-ton truck was trying to do the job of a ten-ton truck. You don't need a major overhaul, but you do need a tune up. So take six weeks off and do nothing." So I did. I read, began an exercise program, took up racquetball, and began to recover.

It wasn't until months later that I realized what really turned it around for me. We owned two Shelties and during this time our female delivered five puppies. My wife and I sat there for four hours acting as midwives helping Amber deliver them. We told her to breathe, "Amber, breathe, now push, whoosh, whoosh, puff, whoosh," and she did. And the puppies arrived.

Every morning for the next eight weeks I would come into the kitchen first thing in the morning, lower the bar of the playpen, and let the puppies out. I would sit on the floor and, when old enough, the pups would run all around and over me, playing and romping and investigating. After a while they'd get tired and fall asleep in my lap. Each day I was seeing new life unfold in front of me. And that's what really rekindled my interest in life again. They brought a new spark to my eyes and a smile to my face.

That's what puppies do.

So do children.

In October of 2001, I spent six days in New York City teaching on loss, grief, and trauma. I also spent hours counseling and listening to the survivors of the World Trade Tower disaster. At the end of each day I was exhausted.

Following this, I flew to another city to teach a marriage seminar. I was very weary and hoping I'd have energy to help the couples there. I received a call from my wife in the middle of the seminar to tell me I was a grandfather. Our first! And we didn't even know this adopted baby girl existed two months before. My energy returned.

Five days later I walked into our daughter's home. When I saw Sheryl holding this tiny baby, there were no words to describe what I felt. I kept saying, "She's so small." What a delight it was to hold her, give her the bottle, and then watch her wrap her little hand around my finger. What a feeling of joy! That's what children bring to your life. Take time to enjoy your child no matter how old he or she is. Our children are the future. Each child can bring a spark to your eyes and a smile to your face. ❖

The reason a dog has so many friends
is that he wags his tail instead of his tongue.
ANONYMOUS

Puppies, Kids, and Anger

It's hard to get angry at a puppy. Or is it? You tell your puppy to do something and he (which of the following pushes your anger button?):

  A. ignores you
  B. looks at you with a "Huh? What'd ya say?"
  C. gives you a look that emphatically says "No!"
  D. hikes its leg and douses your foot
  E. all of the above

Many owners expect instant perfection from their puppy. It won't happen. That's why we call them puppies. These expectations can lead to anger and frustration. And your anger will get through to a puppy just like it does to a child.

Your pup will feel that it's bad and you're pushing it away. Did you know that puppies fear rejection so much that it gets in the way of them learning what you want them to learn? Now, isn't that a hoot! We want our dog to learn but sometimes we get angry. Anger inhibits learning. So we've created the very situation we are trying to get rid of! Our anger creates an emotional response in our pup (it could happen to our children as well). He gets confused, insecure, and anxious.

Or, since dogs love emotion of any kind, he could see your anger as, "Great! I've got him going. I'll just keep this up." Dogs are as attracted to anger as happiness! Emotion of any kind reinforces what your dog was doing. Just like with children, "any attention is better than no attention." Ever thought of that?

Puppies and children are very similar— your anger may provoke anger in them… and then no one wins. ♣

School Daze

THINK BACK TO YOUR YEARS IN GRAMMAR SCHOOL. Remember the teacher who was dull, talked in a monotone, and was *borrrinng*? Sure we all had them. Were we motivated to learn? Did we have that burning desire to explore the subject? I doubt it. If the teacher wasn't excited about the subject, why should we be?

Puppies are no different. A monotone owner that acts like he doesn't have a pulse can put his puppy into a trance. Lack of enthusiasm when you're training your puppy is a downer. It keeps him from learning. You've got to model for your puppy (and your child) how practicing what you're teaching will change their life, turn them into a "Wonder Dog," keep fleas a mile away, and make every cat cower. If you have an enthusiastic attitude, your pup will want to learn. You don't have to act like Bozo the Clown or do cartwheels. All you have to do is smile, grin, clap your hands, say "good dog!", laugh, and be pleasant.

Remember attitude is a chain that ties your dog's performance to you with cast-iron bonds, rubber bands, or silken threads. Ever wonder why your child doesn't jump up and down at some of your suggestions? Delivery is everything. ❧

There is no psychiatrist in the world like a puppy licking your face.

BERN WILLIAMS

Learning Methods

Have you seen the child who gets lost between the front door and the car? Or the one who's sent to his room to clean it and two hours later he's still playing with the toys he's supposed to be putting away? This child gets distracted easily and has a short attention span. He could be a dreamer.

Some puppies are the same. With children and puppies alike, we need to adjust our teaching and instruction per the individual.

If your pup has a long attention span, you can work for longer periods of time without a break. It's the same with a child.

If your pup has a medium attention span, he may need some reminding the next day to reinforce what he learned the day before. Or, perhaps he needs shorter learning sessions. It works the same with your child. He may need more verbal prompting.

And then there's the "short memory pup." A butterfly or cricket grabs his attention. A ten-second teaching time works best along with numerous repetitions. He may forget quickly. He's not dumb, just distracts easily. So give him short parts to remember. Break the task into small steps and eventually he'll put it all together. It's the same with a child. And when your pup or child succeeds, you know what to do—give him praise—enthusiastic praise. Lock it in and you'll both be happy. In order for this to work you'll need to do one other thing—pray for patience!

Positive Reinforcement

Puppies and children who are constantly wanting attention can be obnoxious. They never seem to get enough. The biggest problem is the way they go about getting it! For example, a child may whine or have a tantrum. A puppy may jump up on you.

What do people do with a jumping puppy? They pat it, pick it up, or yell at it and jump away. Every response reinforces the behavior. The puppy gets some kind of attention. Even yelling is better than no attention and jumping away could be a new game. You want to discourage the behavior you don't want, not encourage it. Remember puppies and children are the same—they continue to behave in ways that work for them. Teach your puppy to sit-to-greet people, not jump-to-greet. Reward and reinforce the sitting, not the jumping. And if your pup jumps,

turn around and walk away. Then come back in and repeat the sequence until the pup realizes sitting works, jumping doesn't.

With your child who whines, you can ignore but reinforce non-whining responses or each time they whine they could write, "I will request in a positive tone and will not whine" a dozen times. If there's a tantrum, you can ignore it, get on the floor and have a tantrum with them, or encourage them to have a tantrum and cry louder! Crazy?

23

Perhaps, but it works. When they don't have a tantrum over what usually triggers one, reinforce it. Remember, if what you're doing isn't working now, what have you got to lose?

Learning Curves

Have you had one of those great mornings with your puppy? You know, he was loving, playful, and obedient. He followed every instruction such as sit, lie down, stay, or give. You thought, "Max (the number-one choice for a dog name) is brilliant. He's learning so fast. He's great." And then an hour later he doesn't seem to remember a thing. What happened? Why did he regress? It's time to remember a major fact—he's a puppy. That's all. Learning takes time and practice. Puppies learn continually but sometimes being a puppy takes precedence over learning.

What are your expectations? Do you tend to be a perfectionist? Remember perfect dogs and perfect children don't exist. Give your puppy and your child permission in your heart and mind to make mistakes. Your love and acceptance of them is not based on their perfection.

Mistakes or lapses are not the issue. It's how you respond when they happen. You have a choice to focus on the problem or the solution. Remember, your puppy's and your child's learning depends on *your* teaching ability.

Two of a Kind

Puppies and children are so alike. They look around their world with amazement. "Wow! What a place to explore and conquer." And they both want to feel safe and secure. But, how does this happen?

Enter the world of a puppy. He wants to be led. He wants to know who's in charge of this show. Who can he depend on? You. You're the leader of the pack. Puppies want leadership. They defer to leadership. But as soon as he knows you're the top dog, what's the first thing he does? Of course, he challenges you. He wants to know if you're capable of leading him. He wants reassurance. And his challenge will come at any time, especially when you're tired or frazzled. If you're unable to lead or are inconsistent, your life *will* be miserable. When a puppy controls a person, well, it's not a pretty picture. When your puppy pushes and challenges, gently stand your ground and reaffirm, "I'm the one in charge."

Children will do the same. They will challenge the rules to see if you mean what you say. If you don't reinforce the rules, you both lose. You lose respect, control, and the power to lead your child. Your child loses security and direction.

Let them challenge. That's part of growing up. It's their way of gaining the reassurance they desire. ❧

Having once been punished, dogs remember, but like children,
they hope they won't be caught in the act.

BARBARA WOODHOUSE
No Bad Dogs, The Woodhouse Way

Know Your Puppy, Know Your Child

PRAISE AND APPRECIATION ARE IMPORTANT FOR PUPPIES AND KIDS. But they need to be applied thoughtfully considering the personality of each.

How do you communicate puppy praise? Think about the various ways. You can use light touching, playful petting, a rubdown, an enthusiastic voice, a big smile with an encouraging tone, some games, or even food treats.

When you praise you send a message: "I appreciate what you've done for me." But the way you offer praise makes a big difference. Some dogs and children prefer touch. Others are primarily auditory so they appreciate what you say more than anything else. Try to discover your puppy's (and child's) love language and use it. Some pups aren't tuned into what you say but love the touch. It's the same with children.

Pups and children also vary in their sensitivity. Vigorous rubbing and a loud voice to a soft and sensitive puppy are not really appreciated. To a pup, that's not praise, it's abuse! Ever had a shy puppy? They cower *so* easily. Especially when a loud, large, dominating person approaches. When you loom over this puppy, he feels threatened and uses the CRP approach. You know what that is, don't you? They cower, run, or piddle. But when a person approaches casually, slowly, quietly, and even crouches down on the level with the pup, what a difference. The overbearing threat is gone. And the puppy responds. A loud, excited voice to a shy or introverted child who hates to be the center of attention is perceived the same way. This child appreciates soft praise in private.

If your puppy is already emotionally wired, you don't want to add to this with an excited, exuberant voice. Speaking softly and stroking your pup's ears will get the message across and help to calm him down.

And try to vary your praise for both. If you become predictable, you won't be heard.

Remember the following:

Praise and appreciation need to be given after the act is done, not during it. If you do, they might stop in mid-stream.

Praise should encourage your pup or child to repeat what they just did and feel good about it. ♣

What Do They Hear?

IT'S AMAZING WHAT A PUPPY CAN HEAR. They seem to have a supersonic sense of hearing when you open the refrigerator door or a box of crackers. They can appear at your side instantaneously. Their hearing is *much* better than yours. Your pup can determine the location of a sound in six one-hundredths of a second. Sure, the speed of light is faster, but you and I can't do this. Your pup hears sounds that are farther away—in fact, they can hear sounds that originate more than six times farther away than you can hear. So, if your pup wakes up barking and growling, don't get on his case. He hears something you don't. Be thankful for that. It could save your life some day.

Puppies hear subsonic tones as well as sounds that reach as high as 45,000 vibrations per second. So, don't blow a "silent whistle" too close to them. It's too much.

Here's the big question: If dogs can hear so well, why do their owners yell at them? Ever thought about that?

When you yell at your pup or child you send a message. You've lost control, or you're frustrated, or angry, or... (you fill in the blank). Yelling may intimidate, but it doesn't teach. Yelling may produce fear, but it's not effective. Whether it's a puppy or a child, don't raise your voice, lower it. A firm, low voice does wonders. It works even better if you get up from where you are, go to the pup or child, touch either gently on the shoulder, look them in the eye, and softly communicate what you have to say. This *will* make a difference.

Tune-Up Your Tone

And while you're at it, use the tone of voice to your advantage as well. It can be very effective. Did you know that in a face-to-face message with a person or a pooch, your tone of voice makes up 38 percent of the message? That's five times more impact than content (7 percent). Body language or non-verbal makes up 55 percent.

Are you aware of your tone? You can do wonders with it. When we bought our first Sheltie, the breeder said, "Never strike a dog. Use your tone of voice." I'm always open to a challenge, so I followed the advice. With my tone of voice I could have Prince and his mate, Amber, come running to me, and with a tonal change, they'd stop. It would work even under pressure, like a cat walking in front of them. They would stop and wait until they heard a word with the right tone: "Git um" and off they'd go.

I learned something about myself from my Sheltie pups. They have an addiction—to tennis balls. They want to play all the time and seem to think if I'm not doing something I should entertain them (not much different than our children). I'd be talking on the phone and just before I would hang up, my dog would appear on the scene with a tennis ball in his mouth as though he knew I would be off the phone and available. I wondered, "How does he know? Is it a sixth

forget raising the volume. Use your tone instead. Practice it. Try tape recording your family dinner conversations and listen to your tone. You'll be amazed.

Talk Less, Listen More

One other suggestion: Have you ever caught yourself lecturing your puppy? You know… going on and on and on about what they should be doing, need to do, shouldn't do, etc. Do you really think they're catching all you're saying? We do the same with our children.

There's an approach that parents use quite frequently and to their detriment—*lecturing*. It's when we try to correct a child by teaching, giving all the facts, often pointing out what she's been doing wrong, questioning whether her brain was in gear or not, all the time hoping that this approach will solve the problem once and for all. It's called, "tell them,

sense or ESP?" No, it was my tone that changed and he figured it out. People usually change their tone when they're terminating a call. It took Prince to teach me that.

What about your tone with your child? What is it saying? If your child shows you something they make that they're excited about and you reply with a flat, "That's nice," what does your tone convey? If your child says, "Don't be angry" and you say you're not, perhaps they're hearing something different in your tone. If you want to get a point across, teach them, and they'll shape up." Well, for a student to learn something she has to listen, want to learn, be open to change, and excited about discovering something new. I don't think this is the position of most children when they're being lectured. They're usually waiting out the tirade until you're through.

There's a principle that effective parents have learned to follow. If they want to be heard by their children more, they talk less. The greater the amount of verbiage that comes from us, the more it closes a child's ears and mouth. There's a malady that hits children when we begin to lecture. It's called PLG—Parent Lecture Gaze. Our child's eyes begin to gloss over when we start in, and even more so if he knows it's lecture #17. Oh, he may grunt every four or five minutes just to let us know he's awake but that's nothing more than a reflex. Kids see a lecture as a lone *one-sided* interchange sprinkled

with phrases like, "Now, see here," or "You need to listen, young man," or "And furthermore…"

Parents tell me time and time again they have trouble getting their child to listen. Can you ever really get him to pay attention? Yes, you can. Try the following:

1. Be sure you get your child's attention and maintain eye contact. He needs to listen to you with his eyes since nonverbal communication accounts for 55 percent of a message.

2. If your child is a boy, remember he doesn't hear as well as a girl, so you may need to speak a bit louder.

3. Don't give a big answer to your child's little question.

4. Use the "One word rule." That's right, say one word and no more. If your child comes and drops his coat on the floor or chair, instead of going on with, "How many times have I told you…" and being tuned out, just say, "Coat." If your daughter forgets to turn out the lights, just say, "Lights."

Save your words and you'll have better responses.

And with puppies, just use one word with the right tone. I do this all the time. I get Sheffield's or Aspen's attention using one word with the proper tone and…they mind! ❧

A Guideline for Parents of Pups and Kids

Remember you have:

Two eyes to see; watch more than talk.

Two ears to hear; listen more than speak.

Two legs to run, jump and skip;
play more than work.

Arms to hold, touch and guide;
embrace more than scold.

One mouth; think before words escape lips.

Ain't Misbehavin'

SOME PUPPIES ARE MORE THE "ORAL TYPE" THAN OTHERS. THAT'S NOT MUCH DIFFERENT THAN SOME INFANTS. If it isn't nailed to the floor, it goes into the mouth. A puppy will carry anything it can get a hold of including new shoes, slippers, gloves, important documents, children's toys, car keys, and the list goes on. But…it's not their fault. They were born to chew as a puppy. It's called teething. You know, just like an infant. It's not the puppy's fault for chewing any of these items. He found them because we made them accessible. We didn't put them away. When you find your two-year-old dunking your watch or Canon camera in the toilet, how was your child able to reach them? Hmmmmm. It works both ways.

But what if your pup has your favorite item in his mouth? How do you get it back? Of course, start running to grab it out of his mouth. If you do, just remember, he'll love this. It's his favorite game called "chase." The faster you run, the faster he runs. He thinks this is great. All this attention and he'll do it again the next time.

If you're going to play "chase," have your puppy chase you instead. Run away from him, clap your hands, call him by name, and your puppy will chase you. Take the forbidden object away, praise him for coming and obeying, and then give him a proper object to chew. Now he's getting attention for doing what you want him to do.

Think about your child. Does he get attention for misbehaving? If so, why shouldn't he continue? Children learn to get attention one way or another. Give him attention for doing the right thing and that positive behavior should continue. ❧

Bathroom Basics

WHEN IT COMES TO HOUSEBREAKING A PUPPY, YOU HEAR ALL KINDS OF ADVICE. I've heard some wild suggestions about how to housebreak a dog—such as have a puppy observe an adult going outside to relieve himself and the puppy will follow suit. They call this "modeling." This approach has been suggested with small children as well. After all, don't kids want to imitate grown-ups?

My wife and I raised a profoundly mentally retarded son. At his death at 22 he was about 18 months old mentally. He never was toilet trained. But when he was younger we met with a specialist at the regional center to help us with issues such as toilet training, feeding, etc. I can still remember the suggestion from the specialist (who really didn't have a clue to our son's ability) who said, "Now, Mr. Wright, here's how you can teach Matthew to go to the bathroom. Take him to the toilet, throw in some raisins, and say, 'Now, Matthew, let's play sink the submarines' and you proceed to show him and he will follow your lead." I looked at Joyce, she looked at me, and then we looked at this specialist with a "you've got to be kidding" expression. We bit our tongues and got out of there as fast as we could before we exploded with laughter. That may have worked for some children, but not for Matt. Modeling is a good idea for children…but for puppies?

Some might say use newspapers and let him go inside until he's old enough to hold it. Others say forget the paper. Take him out often enough so he has a favorite spot and when he whimpers or paws at the door, take him out with the words "Let's go potty." Praise him as much as possible when he is successful. In no time, he will know what those words mean.

If he has an accident, clean it up immediately and don't make a big deal over it. Punishing a pup for doing what comes naturally doesn't make sense. If you see your pup walking in circles and starting that familiar squat, rush him outside.

Any dog can have an accident. I mean, if we can why not them? Unfortunately, some accidents are worse than others. I was fishing on a lake with two of my friends and Prince, one of my Shelties, was in our boat. I thought he had gone potty before we left, but something he ate was doing the rumble in his stomach. As the boat sped along, all of a sudden Prince began to pace back and forth near the front of the boat. I knew the signs. I also knew we couldn't get to shore in time. We were in for a disaster! Prince let go. He felt better…we felt sick. Accidents do happen.

Actually, I'm an advocate of PTT—Precision Toilet Training. My dogs, Sheffield and Aspen, are golden retrievers. I'll take them out and say "Potty," but then I'll tell them to go either number one or number two and give them the signs as well. It works great. When we travel or walk the neighborhood, I don't have to be concerned with them doing a potty stop along the way. People are amazed. How did I do this? It was easy. You just catch them in the act, say the words, and give a sign. (Once in a while I'll say "three" and hold up three fingers. The dogs look at me with a "what's that?" expression.) Do this often enough and it locks in. With sit, lie down, stop, or heel, you have to teach them. With this method, they're already in action and you come alongside and attach the commands. It's the old principle that works great with puppies and children—when they're doing what you want, that's when to say something positive. Reinforce what they're doing and give them praise. Are you doing this? It can change their responses and lower your frustration.

After Joyce and I'd been married for a year she said, "Boy, did your mother toilet train you well." I've always wondered what she meant by that. Oh well, at least it carried over to the dogs. ❧

Catch your puppy doing something right and reward it.

Catch your child doing something right and reward him.

Catch yourself doing and saying the right thing to your puppy and child and you'll have your reward.

If your puppy or child does something wrong, don't reward that— redirect them.

How Many Dogs Does It Take to Change a Lightbulb?

GOLDEN RETRIEVER: "The sun is shining, the day is young, we've got our whole lives ahead of us, and you're inside worrying about a silly burned-out lightbulb?"

BORDER COLLIE: "Just one. And I'll replace any wiring that's not up to code."

DACHSHUND: "I can't reach it!!"

TOY POODLE: "I'll just blow in the Border collie's ear, and he'll do it. By the time he finishes rewiring the house, my nails will be dry."

LAB: "Oh, me, me!!! Pleeeeeeze let me change the lightbulb. Can I? Can I? Huh? Huh? Can I?"

COCKER SPANIEL: "Why change it? I can still piddle on the carpet in the dark."

AUSTRALIAN SHEPHERD: "First put all the lightbulbs in a little circle..."

OLD ENGLISH SHEEP DOG: "Lightbulb? Lightbulb? That thing I just ate was a lightbulb?"

CHIHUAHUA: "Yo Quiero Taco Bulb." ❧

OUR PRIDE

Communicate What You Mean

YOU'RE LYING IN YOUR BED AND YOUR PUPPY JUMPS UP ON THE BED. You immediately say, "down." What does he do? He lies down on the bed. He did what you asked even though you probably wanted him to get off the bed. If so, the word is "off." "Off" means "get off." "Down" means "lie down." An obedient dog learns when we use the right words. Say what you mean and mean what you say.

Timing is another factor. You may be able to come back to a child with a corrective response several minutes later, but with a puppy? No way. Correcting or praising needs to happen in the first two seconds after his action or he won't associate what you said with what he did. If you praise before he finishes, why continue?

And give your puppy time to think about what you said. He has to think about it and process the new information. Some parents get their child to respond within a half a second, but not because the child thought about the request and learned from it. It was out of fear, and this inhibits learning in the long run—it erodes their sense of security. And they lose confidence in you as their source of strength. Sure, it's easier to stick to your guns with a puppy. They can't argue back with words. But a child…that's another matter.

What can you do when your child wears you down? Years ago I learned an approach called the *Broken Record Technique*. When someone is trying to persuade you to change your mind, or to purchase something, or to do something, all you have to do is employ the *broken record technique* and you'll win. Most people can't last against this defense. If someone is pressuring you to buy something, and trying to find out the reason why you won't buy it (which you don't have to do and shouldn't give!), all you have to say is, "No, thank you. I'm just not interested," again and again and the other person will give up. If a friend is pressuring you to attend something and you don't want to go, all you have to say is, "Thank you for asking, but I'm unable to attend." Again, you don't have to give your reason.

Let's say you've asked your son to clean his room before he goes over to his friend's house to go swimming. He agreed, but he hasn't done it yet. Jimmy runs by and says: "See ya, Mom. I'm going over to Ken's to swim."

Mom: "Wait up, Jimmy. You said earlier that you would clean your room before you went to Ken's."

Jimmy: "But Mom, I need to leave now. It would take too long to clean it."

Mom: "That may be the case, Jimmy, but feel free to go when your room is clean."

Jimmy: "Mom—Ken called and wants to show me stuff before the others get there."

Mom: "I'm sure he does and feel free to go as soon as your room is clean."

Jimmy: "Why can't I do it later? Other kids get to play first and then they do the work. It's not fair."

Mom: "That may be true, Jimmy, and feel free to go after your room is clean."

Jimmy cleaned his room. ❧

© J. Lamb

NO-K...
society: ...end donation...
Box 102, Hamel, MN 55340

404 Dogs

DOGGUS FRIENDLIUS I play,
chase, jump, dig, bark, and bite.
Assembly (training) required.
Batteries (food) not included.
Health care mandatory. Yearly
Cost: $750 to $3,000.
Additional Recommendations:
I prefer to sleep in the bedroom
with you. Please provide a
minimum of 2 hours a day for
playing, exercise, socialization,
and employment. Education must
include emotional, mental, and
physical stimulation.
Benefits: *I will accept you as you
are, unconditionally love you,
work with you, grow with you,
and together we will form a living,
loving bond.*

BEAGLE PU...
2 Males ...
worm...

43

30 Words

by Gary Stanley

A FEW YEARS BACK, ONE OF THE PROFESSORS AT THE SCHOOL WHERE I TAUGHT volunteered that Nathan, her two-year-old, had a working vocabulary of 25 words. I wasn't quite sure how I was supposed to respond. It was certainly a novel thing to note—so precise and definitive—a celebration of some sort of verbal benchmark. She seemed quite pleased, so I smiled and noted that she and her husband did indeed have a bright boy.

That night I checked out Griffin's working vocabulary—it was 30 words. Griffin is a year or two older than Nathan, but I figured I was in possession of a remarkable bit of news. Probably should have kept it to myself. Probably should have just let it slide—didn't.

At first opportunity, I informed my colleague that Griffin's vocabulary was 30 words. I think I caught her by surprise. She knows Griffin, and after a moment's reflection she congratulated me on that remarkable accomplishment and changed the subject. I felt a bit uneasy after our conversation, sensing that I'd stepped over some invisible boundary seen only by parents of actual children.

That little boy is now in third grade, and his working vocabulary is well beyond numbering—he is indeed a bright boy. Griffin, on the other hand, is still in possession of the same 30-word vocabulary. Turns out he's pretty smart, too—for a dog. He's even done a couple of bit parts for Disney, playing Old Yeller.

At this point, let me ease any parental discomfort you may be experiencing. I know

a dog is not a child. The theological reality is that one has a spirit, and the other doesn't. One is an image-bearer of the Creator, and the other merely a reflection. One has eternity set in his or her heart, and the other has only a vague ache it shares with all creation. Still, the working vocabularies of life can be gleaned both from those who crawl on all fours as well as those who walk on all fours. 🐾

Words to Live By

HAVE YOU HEARD OF THE *INTERNATIONAL DOGGIE DICTIONARY*? Puppies are taught these definitions by their mothers. Here are a few:

Leash. A leash is a strap which attaches to your collar, enabling you to lead your owner where you want to go when you're out for a walk.

Dog Bed. This is any soft, clean surface, such as the white bedspread in the guest room.

Drool. Drool is what you do when your owner has food and you don't. Allow the saliva to drip into a pool on the floor.

Sniff. Sniffing is a social custom to use when you greet other dogs. Place your nose as close as possible to the other dog's rear and inhale deeply. Repeat several times, or until your owner makes you stop.

Guests. Guests are people who come to your home to see you whine at the table, bark loudly, jump up on women wearing pantyhose, and do other tricks which you wouldn't think of doing just for the family.

Deafness. This is a malady which affects dogs whose owners want them to come in when they want to stay out.

Fence. A game of skill, the object of which is to get on the other side as quickly as possible.

Sofa. Sofas are to dogs what napkins are to people.

By the way, what are *you* teaching your child? Make a list of ten words you or your child use—ask your child what these words mean. You may be surprised! ❧

True Dog Confessions

THERE IS SOMETHING I HAVE TO CONFESS. I never, ever listen to your whole sentences. It's not that I don't care what you're saying, it's just that I'm smart enough to know the difference between key words and fluff. My mind quickly filters out the extra words and I connect the key words with subtle nonverbal cues. *I hope I haven't hurt your feelings.*

I do have one small favor to ask of you to help from confusing me: please don't say the command twice within seconds. For example, please don't say "sit," then two seconds later yell "sit" again just because I'm not responding as fast as you'd like.

I can become confused when you "double talk" to me. It sounds like a totally different command, like "sit-sit."

For instance, wouldn't you become confused if someone someone started started talking talking to to you you like like this this. *I think you get the message.*

How often do we repeat the same words over and over again to our children? Could it be we teach them *not* to respond the first time around? It's something to think about. ❧

Happy Homecomings

by Max Lucado

FOR THE LAST 20 YEARS, I'VE WANTED A DOG. A BIG DOG. But there were always problems. The apartment was too small. The budget was too tight. The girls were too young. But most of all, Denalyn was unenthusiastic. Her logic? She'd already married one slobbering, shedding beast, why put up with a second? So we compromised and got a small dog.

I like Salty, but small dogs aren't really dogs. They don't bark; they yelp. They don't eat; they nibble. They don't lick you; they sniff you. I like Salty, but I wanted a real dog. A man's-best-friend type of dog. A fat-pawed, big-eating, slurp-you-on-the-face type of dog you could saddle or wrestle or both.

I was alone in my passion until Sara was born. She loves dogs. And the two of us were able to sway the household vote. Denalyn gave in, and Sara and I began the search. We discovered a woman in South Carolina who breeds golden retrievers in a Christian environment. From birth the dogs are surrounded by inspirational music and prayers. (No, I don't know if they tithe with dog biscuits.) When the trainer told me that she had read my books, I got on board. A woman with such good taste is bound to be a good breeder, right?

So we ordered a pup. We mailed the check, selected the name Molly, and cleared a corner for her dog pillow. The dog hadn't even been born, and she was named, claimed, and given a place in the house.

After a month in our house she ran away. I came home one night to find the place unusually quiet. Molly was gone.

She'd slipped out unnoticed. The search began immediately. Within an hour we knew that she was far, far from home. Now, if you don't like pets, what I'm about to say is going to sound strange. If you do like pets, you will understand.

You'll understand why we walked up and down the street, calling her name. You'll understand why I drove around the neighborhood at 10:30 P.M. You'll understand why I put a poster in the convenience store and convened the family for prayer. (Honestly, I did.) You'll understand why I sent e-mails to the staff, asking for prayers, and to her breeder, asking for advice. And you'll understand why we were ready to toss the confetti and party when she showed up.

Here is what happened. The next morning Denalyn was on her way home from taking the girls to school when she saw the trash truck. She asked the workers to keep an eye out for Molly and then hurried home to host a mom's prayer group. Soon after the ladies arrived the trash truck pulled into our driveway, a worker opened the door, and out bounded our dog. She had been found.

When Denalyn called to tell me the news, I could barely hear her voice. It was Mardi Gras in the kitchen. The ladies were celebrating the return of Molly.

This story pops with symbolism. The master leaving his house, searching for the lost. Victories in the midst of prayer. Great things coming out of trash. But most of all: the celebration at the coming home. That's something else you have in common with Molly—a party at your homecoming.

By that moment only one bag will remain. Not guilt. It was dropped at Calvary. Not the fear of death. It was left at the grave. The only lingering luggage will be this God-given longing for home. And when you see Him, you'll set it down. Just as a returning soldier drops his duffel when he sees his wife, you'll drop your longing when you see your Father. Those you love will shout. Those you know will applaud. But all the noise will cease when he cups your chin and says, "Welcome home." And with scarred hand he'll wipe every tear from your eye. And you will dwell in the house of your Lord—forever. ❧

What I Learned from My Dog

Never pass up the opportunity to go for a joyride.

Allow the experience of fresh air and the wind in my face to be pure ecstasy.

When loved ones come home, I will always run to greet them.

Let others know when they have invaded my territory.

Take naps and stretch before rising.

Run, romp, and play daily.

Eat with gusto and enthusiasm.

Be loyal.

Never pretend to be something I am not.

If what I want lies buried, I will dig until I find it.

When someone is having a bad day, I will be silent, sit close by, and nuzzle him gently.

Avoid biting when a simple growl will do.

On hot days, drink lots of water and lie under a shady tree.

When you're happy, dance around and wag your entire body. 🐾

© J.LAMB

© J.Lamb '88

A Dog's-Eye View of Obedience Class

THE OBEDIENCE TESTS...WILL BORE YOU TO DEATH, BUT WITH YOUR OWN VARIATIONS YOU CAN PLAY FOREVER AND SCORE YOUR OWN WAY:

HEEL ON LEAD: ...Walk as slowly as you can, then spring forward with all your weight. If your handler falls flat on his face, you score 25 points.

RECALL: When [your handler] shouts at you, assume rock deafness... On no account sit in front of your handler, because he will only make you heel...25 points if handler loses voice.

RETRIEVE THE DUMBBELL: ...On no account fetch it back, because he will only throw it away again. If he wants the stupid piece of wood let him fetch it himself; you will be helping to train him not to throw away things he really wants... You get 5 points every time handler gets dumbbell.

SIT: ...Stay one inch away from the ground at the back end.

CONCLUSION: ...Do any exercise you choose perfectly! This will leave your handler thinking that the earlier mistakes were his fault, and he will take you to training class week after week.

Do you ever wonder if our own children respond the same way? Hmmm. ❧

Heroes — Both of Them

JIM AND RICK WERE BORN 20 YEARS APART, YET WERE SO SIMILAR. Each was firstborn with all the unique qualities of this birth order position—achievers, leaders, capable, and outgoing. But each was a typical youngster. There were accidents in their toilet training, food spills, squabbling with siblings, wandering too far from home, and testing limits to see if Mom or Dad meant what they said. In both families the parents were fair, disciplined where necessary, and encouraged each to do his best and serve others. Compassion for those who hurt was a consistent theme of their upbringing. The message they were taught could be summarized by "You've been given a life. Use it to help others."

Each had their time in the doctor's office for checkups, bruises, and shots but fortunately no broken bones. Both were addicted to sports, especially football. One was a great passer and the other an adept receiver. Too bad they never played on the same team.

Upon graduation from school Jim became a firefighter in New York City, the fulfillment of a boyhood dream. He quickly rose through the ranks because of his ability and leadership.

Rick went into Search and Rescue work and completed his training at the top of his class. Soon he was the one called upon whenever these services were needed. He settled in Florida and was assigned to the Dade County Fire Department. Two public servants who were born at different times in different places and were working so far from one another. On several occasions Rick was asked to go to New York to assist in Search and Rescue. Every time he and Jim ended up working together. They made a very efficient team and developed a close working relationship. Jim looked forward to these occasions so much that he began entertaining thoughts of how he could work more with Rick and his team. But as time went on each became busier in their section of the country and the years slid by since they had worked together. What were the chances that their paths would cross again one day?

On September 11, 2001, a nightmare erupted in Manhattan. Two planes gouged the Twin Towers and flames consumed structure and people alike. Hundreds of firefighters responded and, without a thought for their safety, began the arduous climb up hundreds of stairs. With heavy equipment and crowded stairwells, they struggled upward as frightened office workers streamed past them, fleeing for their lives. As Jim and the others reached one of the floors, they could see injured people amongst the chaos. All Jim could think of was helping and rescuing those stranded in pain. Some were taken down the stairwell by rescue workers. A few minutes later, though, the building shuddered. Then it collapsed. There was nothing but dust, debris, and darkness. It was reminiscent of the early words of Genesis, "And the earth was formless and void, and darkness was over the surface of the deep" (Genesis 1:2, NASB).

Soon all that could be seen was thick stifling clouds rising from the rubble. More than 300 rescue workers were entombed in this pile.

Rick and his team arrived on the scene three days later. They were pressed into service immediately searching for survivors. But it wasn't easy going. Most of the rescuers had masks to protect them from the dust and toxins in the air. Rick didn't. And soon his feet were cut and bleeding because of the glass and metal. He didn't have the protection boots.

You see, Rick was a golden retriever.

He had been trained to find survivors. Unfortunately, in the rubble, there were none, only the dead. Soon he and other Search and Rescue dogs were discouraged. Taught to bark upon finding someone alive, he or the other dogs would just sit down upon making a discovery.

It happened on the third morning. As the rescue workers transported rubble out of the large pit the dogs were searching, Rick came on alert. He found someone. From the uniform, it was obviously a firefighter. His handler noticed he was sitting but this time he was pawing and whining. He kept pawing even though it meant more pain to his sore feet. The fireman was uncovered. It was Jim. While Rick would have easily recognized Jim when he was alive, did he recognize him now? Was that why he pawed and whined? I don't know, but there was some connection there. As Jim was lifted out and a flag draped over his body, other firefighters stood in a line while he was carried out. Rick followed right behind. A hush came over the scene at Ground Zero. One hero was being carried out. One was following in silent tribute as if to say, "We're together again. You've given your all. I'll stay and keep working."

Jesus said, "Greater love has no man than this, that one lay down his life for his friends" (John 15:12).

This story is dedicated to those faithful parents who raise their children to think of others in a selfless way.

It is also dedicated to all those rescue workers in New York City who gave their all in seeking to help others. May we never forget their efforts on September 11, 2001. ❧

Acknowledgments

"Your Puppy's Brain" is adapted from *What Do Dogs Know* by Stanley Coren and Janet Walker (New York: The Free Press, 1997), p. 6.

"A Message from Your Puppy" is adapted from *Hi, It's Me, Your Dog!* by Lisa Mendosa (Clovis, CA: Quill Drive Books, 2000), pp. 7–10 and *What Do Dogs Know* by Stanley Coren and Janet Walker (New York: The Free Press, 1997), p. 20.

"Puppies, Kids, and Anger" is adapted from *Bonnie Bergin's Guide to Bringing Out the Best in Your Dog* by Bonnie Bergin with Robert Aquinas McNally (New York: Little Brown & Co., 1995), pp. 150–152.

"School Daze" is adapted from *Catch Your Dog Doing Something Right* by Krista Cantrell (New York: A Plume Book, 1998), p. 71.

"Learning Methods" is adapted from *Catch Your Dog Doing Something Right* by Krista Cantrell (New York: A Plume Book, 1998), pp. 25–30; 78–80, and *Puppies! Why Do They Do What They Do?* by Penolope Milne (Irvine, CA: Bowtie Press, 2001), pp. 13–15.

"Know Your Puppy, Know Your Child" is adapted from *Bonnie Bergin's Guide to Bringing Out the Best in Your Dog* by Bonnie Bergin with Robert Aquinas McNally (New York: Little Brown & Co., 1995), pp. 128–130.

"What Do They Hear?" is adapted from *Loving Your Child Is Not Enough* by Nancy Samalin (New York: Penguin Books, 1998), p. 14.

"Guidelines for Parents of Pups and Kids" is adapted from *Catch Your Dog Doing Something Right* by Krista Cantrell (New York: A Plume Book, 1998), p. 19.

"Communicate What You Mean" is adapted from *Catch Your Dog Doing Something Right* by Krista Cantrell (New York: A Plume Book, 1998), pp. 100–101, and from *Parenting with Love and Logic* by Foster Cline, M.D. and Jim Fay (Colorado Springs, CO: NavPress, 1990), p. 83.

"Doggus Friendlius" is adapted from *The Dog Whisperer* by Paul Owens with Norma Eckroote (Holbrook, MA: Adams Media Corp., 1999), p. 6.

"30 Words" is adapted from *What My Dog Has Taught Me About Life* by Gary Stanley (Tulsa, OK: Honor Books, 1999), pp. 10–12.

"Words to Live By" is adapted from *The Dogs of Our Lives* compiled by Louise Goodyear Murray (Seacaucus, NJ: Carol Publishing Group, 1995), pp. 22–24.

"True Dog Confessions" is adapted from *Hi! It's Me, Your Dog!* by Lisa Mendoza (Clovis, CA: Quill Driver Books, 2000), p. 56.

"Happy Homecomings" is adapted from *Traveling Light* by Max Lucado (Nashville: Word Publishing Group, 2001), pp. 151–157.

"What I Learned from My Dog" is adapted from *Animal Blessings, Prayers and Poems Celebrating Our Pets* by June Cotner (San Francisco: Harper San Francisco, 2000), p. 3.

"A Dog's-Eye View of Obedience Class" is adapted from *277 Secrets Your Dog Wants You to Know* by Paulette Cooper and Paul Noble (Berkeley, CA: Ten Speed Press, 1995), p. 14.

"A Blessing for a Child's New Pet" is adapted from *Animal Blessings, Prayers and Poems Celebrating Our Pets* by June Cotner (San Francisco: Harper San Francisco, 2000), p. 156.